LIFE SENTENCES

Life Sentences

Poems

James McGonigal

RED SQUIRREL PRESS

First published in 2023 by Red Squirrel Press
36 Elphinstone Crescent
Biggar
South Lanarkshire
ML12 6GU
www.redsquirrelpress.com

Layout, design and typesetting by Gerry Cambridge
e: gerry.cambridge@btinternet.com

ISBN: 978 1 913632 56 4

A CIP catalogue record for this book is available from
the British Library.

Red Squirrel Press are committed to a sustainable future.
This publication is printed in the UK by Imprint Digital
using Forest Stewardship Certified paper.
www.digital.imprint.co.uk

Contents

BLUE

MAKING TRACKS

BACK TO THE WALL

The Walk

Tears, restrained, still brim towards falling.
A man and a woman were walking,
emotion hidden in their forward steps.

The path rose and fell across fields.
All around them a harvest of something
to be said before reaching the town.

Past and future carried without effort,
so it seemed. But hearts beat deep.
Is there birdsong? Is that fluttering?

A sky. A tree. A gate.

My Father's Letters

Our sycamore has posted
old news to the ground, though other trees
have still a few bright things to say.

What happened to my father's letters?
Early birds shifting between branches
brought his handwriting to mind,

its loops and steadiness,
a pleasing dance centred between
the envelope's right angles. Burnt maybe

to check her sisters' giggling searches
when my mother left for work. Flames
flick each curling sheet

to a whisper, while morning frost
glints along the railway tracks that link
her mining town to his.

Sunday Best

Graves of father and mother
in the west and the east
of a small country.

Does distance matter after all
to the hand that writes it out
or eyes that read?

First light today weaves threads
across everyone's shoulders
like a good coat.

Peace-keeper

Posture and gesture
in a garden: the leaves bend
to meet each other's foreheads

talking closely. Back home from
the outside world we too should reach
out to trees and bushes

waiting for us, and try to grasp
their sign language—
twig tap sip dripdrop.

There's a month of mornings
in those holly berries warning us:
red, and red, and red.

Do you not hear them there
behind their palisade
expecting to fall?

One wet leaf at a jaunty angle,
a beret on our garden buddha's
bald head,

is keeping the peace.

Small Talk

They talk in touch and I half-understand
leaves and stems at their green business
of never turning their back on a neighbour.

There's a dialect called stretch which they tend
to use in the home. It's more subtle and earthy.
But if you can manage touch you'll get by.

When you sit here and listen for hours
or even lay one ear to the ground
whatever it is that you think you are hearing

is only a glance to get you interested.
It's probably better to perambulate.
A gently rolling motion often helps.

And Counting

For months I have studied
       the maple tree, planted
that first year we came.

From baby fingernails
       scratching for purchase
on March air—to the open

palms of summer outstretched
       to catch raindrops—and now
these weather-beaten hands

on crisp November grass.
       I can count on ten fingers
those leaves that still cling

to the maple tree.

Ghost Gardener

The soldier at my back some afternoons
digging south of the Wall
is wary how this spade shines—stainless
fist of a god unearthing what's to come.
He seems more content
listening to my mattock dunt
like a workmate's grunt.

Green of young garlic delights him,
and elder blossom, bean flowers.
Both of us are happy then to persevere
till dusk and moon-breath.
Spring frosts are one worry on this ridge.
Behind us, not far west, the sea
is grinning, or girning. We'll soon see.

Days On the Wall

And the day so blue—wide-eyed but

worried and brisk as a wing-flicker

And the day so grey—one indrawn breath

of the grass thinking somebody's there

And the day—half-blind feeling its way

through flakes that tweak the eye and ear

And the day bending forward to haul

out of the well this morning's peculiar sky

And the nights here the longest on earth watching

stars watching me watching out for them shooting

Time of Fever

That day the fever turned a Mondrian shade of blue—
I thought they were selling the air above me
and wanted the sale to go through.

Green lights were shining in bushes where sparrows
switched on little torches of sound. Sweat's coat
was buttoned at my throat.

We stood on a bridge. Still waters were balancing
their tray of moonlight where two stars
blinked—ice cubes in a glass.

And further on we passed an empty site—road-
widening operations. Yellow rough cut stone
and sorry earth that was crushed and torn.

Living Through It

From skull to gut to calves
it takes its course the way ditchwater
runs after the bend of its road.

An avant-garde composer
is conducting your dreams—night music
for ten-pin bowling quartet.

How long will it last?
Ditchwater sunk two inches deeper into silt,
that's one sign.

When you wake at five
and walk out in the garden to discover a frog
lounging against the cool lip

of the garage floor,
and looking exactly like a spray-tanned scrotum
although you've never seen one,

that's another sign.
But only that you're still not altogether
through the worst.

Nights

What are nights for?
Nights are when we leave.
They come, they take us
Where time turns over.
They are to be absent in:
Where can we hide in thin air
But the night?

Ah, resolving that question
Brings the paramedic or care worker
In their Good Morning colours,
Pushing open the door
To touch one bare shoulder.

Release of Prisoners

How could we have held clouds in both hands
and wrung them out like dishcloths? Our children
woke with snowflakes on their brows.

Can I return to the main point of this illness,
the immediate wound, after some attempts
to stop its tongue of blood?

Starlight must have blessed the skin
and broken it—or voices just outside the tent
have sung us wide awake.

Prose

Is moving on slowly each morning.
I am rising reluctantly to its occasion.
This is no dream, it represents daily life
but wipes the dust from all of its surfaces,
worried by what visitors might think.

My hand like a hoover grieves to and fro
over carpets whose colours
are being beaten to death.

Good Reason

I dreamt last night about Les Murray (who in life translated
bat-flicker and bat-morse, who slipped and split his skull
wide open in the shower, who read his poems fast
in the Glasgow Art School lecture room, both
school and poet fragments now alas).

He was writing a poem in one stanza, tapering
like a knife blade to the page foot. Then
stopped upon a single word. Its theme
was unclear, but could it be that
silent nick of the final word
cutting the page? Overleaf
red was already pulsing
on the sheet. Often the
blood behind a poem
is hidden from its
writer and for
good reason.
Was that
what the
dream
said?

Anniversary

I saw many things done by heart—
days were counted on an abacus of mesh,
the wire made up a crossword minus clues,
men wore walkie-talkies like campaign medals

while we longed to be where fish drift
between weeds, to speak in water vowels
and master the diphthongs of silt.
The river spilled night from its haversack

and packed instead reflections of three deer
at first light, hooves in mud, drinking.
A boy with shaven head saw this
with his own eyes, he told us.

Writing the Asylum

Gains and Losses

Recovery was looking out after a snowfall—
every single bush and fence-post overnight
had come to life in its glow.

And falling ill the second time was like
a snowfall too—each branch and wall appeared
the same, and not the same

in glints of light. They say that it was 'Overstudy'
brought me here. True, figures always charmed me
more than facts.

Now I can total sixteen black marks still visible
on the lawn. Each night I close my ledger of a day
and turn to sleep. Bodies nearby

and boughs stretched white and stark. The moon,
that book-keeper, tallies each silver minute
on fingers of twig.

(1904)

Beside Herself

Did you ever wake
in the small hours
in the half-glow
half-dark and
see with a start

yourself asleep
in the next bed
your other self
lost in her
haplessness

might you not
unrestrained
rise to take
hold of the neck
and choke her fantasies?

We can review
even now this patient's
cast of complexion
surface of tongue
digestive details

and so forth—
but merest hints only
at the love affair
tormenting her.
Lost altogether the hours

of a grim passage
Oban to Glasgow
one daughter shamed
or shameless
raving at waves

her father restless
up on deck
beside himself
with November clouds
boiling astern.

Good nurses chosen
in part for angelic
looks and stout arms
(some of them Highland
lassies) helped.

In barely a week
'Relieved' she returned
to the town
to the glances
to her single bed.

Does agony ever
fade like the ink
on her case notes,
so grey and thin now
that we strain to read?

(1843)

Absent for Some Time

We were two loners or losers who found ourselves sat on the back row of Ordinary English Lit in the Fore Hall of Glasgow University, full of braying first-years trying to impress each other in private-school voices, or so it seemed—me after a 'signally unimpressive start, Mr McGonigal' in French and Spanish and best not to mention Political Economy. This was my second chance.

His story was deflected, self-deprecating in a West of Scotland-Irish manner, pleasant but distant. I think his name was Michael. We got on. Then one day he was gone, back to Gartnavel which he had mentioned once. I wonder now if it might have been shock therapy had distanced him. One of the poems we were lectured on was Robert Lowell's in his asylum days about a violent man lulled by a lobotomy.

He asked me to his flat just once before he left, wanted to lend me a book of Andalusian-Arabic lyrics (*Colección Austral*, 1959), its pages already slightly foxed. Where had he come across it? Did he know Spanish too? Ground floor room in a largish cream-painted villa above the Kelvin's river gorge, so deep that its bankside trees stood eye-to-eye with his window. He never came back to university.

Or maybe I just always missed him in the crowds. So here the book is still, its pages even browner, like autumn-term leaves of 1966. Its poems are all ghazals, those haiku-like laments in the Persian manner. I made a version of one of them:

Do you think my eyes burn,
bare windows for hours in the dark,
without you?

I lie still as a branch,
the distant moon shining all night
through my body.

But my Spanish has gone and I can't find the original Andalusian
poet, nor even the little poetry magazine where I am almost certain
that this translation of a translation was published years later.

(1966)

The Height and Depth of It

I needed to climb
the slope of Gartnavel
to survey across bare winter trees
to the line of his third-floor flat

where the old poet mentioned
one of his aunts abandoned 'in care'—
the villain of the piece her husband
smooth-faced and cynical.

Through the balcony window
the crenellations that I always took
for rooftop features on facing villas
must have been Gartnavel

which he never named
and which I did not pursue
sensing a no-go area
and emotion running deep.

Years later he wrote that poem
about gazing westwards at sunset
from a city balcony away out to the Firth
and then his glance swings

east to the new Gartnavel General's
concrete and glass ablaze in reflected gold
with lines of patients clambering
down this vertical inferno

clinging to their knotted bed-sheets. A vision
not devoid of hope? At this height today
beside the fenced-off dank East Wing
I thought it possible, yes, that here

he had once sat with his aunt among the poor.

(2022)

LIFE SENTENCES

Walking beside me in a dream, not touching,
you asked whether I really understood that this
        was a life sentence.

West wind, wet wind, is bending and polishing
        the holly boughs.

Always look in a baby's eyes; always breathe
in a baby's ear; always smell a baby's skin.

Regarding magpies, look but don't trust.

It is difficult to write two sentences at the same time,
        but not impossible, so long as they do not merge.

The second curse involved feathers.

I was using a dead man's paper and pen to write
        an account of his death in my normal handwriting.

White shirts are haunted by the ghost of sweat.

Years ago he told me what it was like
        flying upside down.

Middle-aged trousers hang in your wardrobe
        like tubas awaiting their promised concerto.

We walk through sunlit rooms this morning
        to the fridge-hum of expectation.

I stood at the crossroads wondering
        why it reminded me of hair.

Mistakes in my writing I always attempt
        to scrape clean, with imperfect success.

On the hottest days, our pavement shadows
seem to scrabble for somewhere cool and dark
        with blackened hands.

I just don't want to draw a line under those thick necks
      of geese eager to dip into northern waters.

The old Frenchman mistook me for someone else,
shook hands vigorously then apologised, staring
      right into my eyes.

The pattern on this carpet has a secret plan
      for the next decade.

A journey's journal—page after page after
      page of *Paradise Mislaid*.

Hills under mist, the curve of them,
      their spectrum of silvers, the shades of them.

There are many who fall asleep miles from the one
      they love best—and some who still lie there awake.

In time we come to appreciate the qualities
of darkness: its colour, tone, pitch and so forth,
          its forthrightness.

We wake and start to walk upon its surface,
          getting the earth rolling.

She was the kind of woman who lived
          much of her life in italics.

Birds were up and about their usual piecework,
          stitching earth to air.

When I showed him the letter that said
I was clear of the cancer, he pointed out
          that the date was wrong.

Who was it passed me just now,
          her coat brushing my hand?

By a trick of the light her face half in shadow
    looked something like mine.

Walking on the earth we sometimes remember
    people in the earth.

That woman with the unattractive voice has written
    some gorgeous poems, it's true.

This clear weather tells us that our daily lives
    proceed mainly through mist.

You need to create some space for yourself,
    the poet in his linen jacket advised me.

An envelope is the heart's haversack, of course.

That tree raising its hand at the end of the road
    wants to ask the sky a question.

His hair, when I met him years later,
looked like an emulsion brush—
            his whitewashed life, no doubt.

At a certain age, I decided to accept
            the consequences of every move she made.

The girl on the train was wearing hiking boots,
            but travelling in courteous company.

When the time came to adjust the blinds,
sweet daylight filled the bedroom's cup
            to overflowing.

In another life, I will have wanted to engineer
            time-travel in a complex Latin tense.

Now that your children are holding their own
sons and daughters, it's time for another chapter
            in the *History of Arms and Legs*.

Old newsreels are grainy with brick-dust and blood.
At 40 I twigged that I would die too—by now
    just a touch late in the day.

BLUE

Inside the Rain

A room that we enter   without asking permission
curious to count   not drops but the scalps
bent to avoid being   pierced by hail.

This mossy sofa is   just what we're used to,
unsettling down   for the night. A black
window declares   how far from us the azure is.

Down the wide strath   there's never a glint
escapes from swollen   banks of burns and
shaded linns.   Will it stop raining soon?

Clouds extend   their palms to be read.

Blue's Anatomy

(Father Hopkins on Holiday)

Doing its losing   its long fall
after snow the blue sky is looking
down-cast   as that whole tree
after last night's frost this morning's
sun began to melt—   at one touch
a leaf downpour
masking the ground at its foot

recalling brown and purple flakes
in diamond-tapered fields one time
            and the near valley
showered with a bluish damp cobalt
poured on the hills   clouds
milky-blue or brown-sail coloured

when he and I walked over to Holywell
and bathed and returned
joyously   water clear as glass
trembling at the surface
from the deep force of its springs

eternity in spring its time in spring
its thoughts buoyant and abundant—
before my eyes recovered   discipline.

***

[48]

I walked over hills where great and vivid Alpine violets
grew on the little brows of grass between shale landslips.
The glacier was painful to look at in the blazing sunlight,
haggard and chipped—a hollow shield its upper member,
and its lower a long tongue of plough-land sloping away.

I noticed these 'twin' glaciers were two descending limbs
of one. The gut all rounded up, but hollowed and rugged
like dog teeth on its upper range; the lower like deep flesh-
cuts where we see the blood flush and come welling out.

Then into the blue tent of a grotto which changed to lilac
further in. At the entrance, daylight glazes its groins with
gleaming rose-colour. The ice inside is of a branchy wiry
texture—one tiny piece pressed against the wall will stick
as if caught by a magnet. A dark guide showed us all this.

***

Susan Bond is married (to Mr. Pooley).
Mrs. Beechey is dead about three weeks.
Baillie is threatened with consumption
and has been spitting blood: he is ordered
south and is going up the Nile. On Sunday
Nov. 22 Frederick Rymer died a holy death
at Pau. He was for a short time a pupil of mine.

***

Under a dark sky walking by the river

where all was sad-coloured and the colour
caught the eye   red and blue of stones
in the river beaches brought out by
                    patches of white-blue snow—
namely snow quite white and dead
                    and yet it seems as if
some blue or lilac screen masked it
somewhere between it and the eye:
                    I have often noticed this
where snow lies the damasking of white light
and silvery shade may be watched
till brightness and glare is   all lost
in a perplexity of shadow
                    and in the whitest of things
the sense of white is lost.

                    ***

A calm sea with little walking wavelets edged
with fine eyebrow crispings, and later nothing
but a netting or a chain-work over the surface
—until even that vanished into a smoothness
marbly and perfect.

and between just-corded nearsides of waves
rising like fishes' backs and breaking with a
darker blue the pale blue of that wider field,
in the sleek hollows shone out golden combs
—reflections from chalk cliffs—oh England.

Distances were shades of blue without haze,
and trees at a distance in the glare appeared
pale yet distinct. Wheat-fields bluish below
but now warm green in the ear—a sundown
peach-coloured, with gilded masses of cloud

which later became finer and smaller

scattering all away—

the heat has gone.

Peerie Poet

He wore a child's head, tilted
at elders to catch
pitches and vowels and turn them
in the road of his mouth.

Next the gab of porridge: plappers,
spoon scrapings. Monday rattles
the latch and Tuesday strides in.
Saturday puffed tobacco rings.

Clouds leaning in
to the lugs of Hoy
spoke in a different
tongue entirely

that could anchor the heart,
or cast off with the sigh
of smoke curling early
from his kitchen fire.

Like Grass Blades

This longing for extension into life—
how your new music should recall

noise it is kin to—traffic shuffle silence ker-
fuffle shouts in fog

noises that fill the world itself stuck to its surface
like the grass blades blown

across fields sticking to her canvas as she paints.
So he said, adding that he owned

two more Joan Eardleys: 'Setting Sun & Stacks' (1956)
and 'Stacks at Evening' (1957).

So those blades of grass are real then…?
Well yes of course, and no.

And concrete poetry too should seek its own extensions
into the life of noises, things, shards,

sidelong looks—all of it embodied there
before our eyes and ears.

Easter: The Esk

Three roads wind down to Langholm
that sits in a valley
like water in a bowl.

Which way to *the fount from whose channel*
by a resolute habit of the will we can clear away
the litter that obstructs the water of life.

Esk over boulders,
Wauchope fleetfoot, in confluence
clattering by your grave.

Awkwardly polished surfaces glance.
A proportion of pearls only.
The transparency choke-full of hair-pin bends.

Esk water round the river bend
fetching and carrying the sky.

Solway Elegy

Just clearing the throat recalls dead men:
we speak and they draw a chair to the fire,
finding their spirits vexed by our plight
and human again

back in Dumfries—earthen jug that pours
its milk out into silver bowls; where onshore
winds lace merse-land crops with salt
for beasts and men.

Grain merchant here, you knew the rules
of a market town, like its building stone,
are firm yet friable, catching light like gold
—to take or lend?—

and seeing uprightness in downright folk
(their flaws your own) you found a faith in what
they'd seldom read: that final clause in the deed
from heaven.

Later you'd take your stick and walk the dog
under the air where constellations clicked
on their ancient abacus (whose hand?)
and then

autumn times winter made a double frost
that sparkled true: Christ laid out on a bolster
dead as your father was, or you—
and rose again.

That's what we breathe: astonishing air.
From Galilee to Glencaple thrawn geese fly
to feed on silt where waves meet reeds
and bend

aside and drift. Unlikely conversationalists
born in the same town, forty years apart—my own uncertain
clever Irish stock, your pugnacious Protestant heart—
yet friends

reading each other's text with the whole mind,
puzzling out senses only poets find.
The minister missed the point today
or leaned

away from coffin, sun and spade.
The closed book of your life, old friend,
was only a draft to be read and remade
yet again

or, in financial terms, the sum to be re-presented
where sheets of light unfold on Galloway hills
and words in a different accent fall
like hail, or grain.

(For Kirkpatrick Dobie, 1908–1999)

With Finnian at His Bright House

Bewildering as light is off the firth, but I could
say his name at least. Come from the west,
he honoured our world with wonders.

There were riddles in a far-travelled face,
snow cloud of hair, a brow like the sea,
hands that spoke different languages.

I am lost for words when I listen again.
At other times forget even to notice that he is
no longer here. How did I lose sight of that

white head in the crowd? I was busy
with other business. One by one we flew
from his fingers like grain—

in dribs and drabs trudged back to life again,
woke with no hand touching the shoulder
to starlight or daylight. Good morning, whatever.

He told us faith is always vanishing, behind
the craig, beyond those rowan trees—pursue, pursue
like hunters do.

With him the memory of everything's a river.
We gathered on its shingle banks to hear
old words dipped clean.

The Half-Awake Soul

The years of my soul have passed
like the warmth of a bed
under sheets of moonlight or rain.
The length of my soul has turned over
from one side to the other.

The best months were spent in silence,
they were passing over into silence.
I'll say no more about that
breath silvering life's mirror
nor tell who was glimpsed there.

I remember whole weeks passed at ease
stretched out on the new grass in May,
or awake as the sea is now
turning waves to a lather of light
in the channels of night.

The best days all had their moments
caught in birdsong or bird flight.
The last look of a cloud leaving the hill behind.
Ourselves making little of it,
turning back to the work of tomorrow.

The years of my soul have come to this
chill morning in a long bed.
Under a duvet of sunlight or snow,
is there strength enough in ankle and thigh
down narrow paths to go?

Is This How They Watch Us

Is this how they watch us, the disappeared,
on indigo Zoom? It's not our heads or hair
that move them, nor eyes obscurely meeting
theirs or glancing at some distraction

but what is visible beyond—new shades of
emulsion, pictures askew, the cat asleep, how
can it doze so long, whiskers and tortoiseshell—
all of those otherlife details,

blue cup minus handle still used to hold pencils,
her money-jar, two porcelain doves pecking
around a carriage clock. Clock-hands often
point out different zones.

Tuning in to our talk, they're glad to see bodies
at home, and with children unborn back then
watching the screen as teenagers do, wary
but unaware of what's to come.

Catching the names of some not here. Maybe
they'll make the next Zoom. Bye then, bye—
Speak soon! Leave. Familiar faces
eclipsed—until the next

random resurrection.

MAKING TRACKS

Up the Gulf of Yedo, quite near the shore…

I heard ecstasies, all over the deck

Our throbbing progress

The first thing that impressed me on landing was that
there were no loafers

Approaching Summer: With Isabella Bird in Japan

The day soft and grey,
a little faint blue sky, no
surprises except...!

Far above any
possibility of height,
a vast cone of snow
curved skywards out of sea mists
then, like a vision, vanished.

Air and water both
motionless—pale grey startled
by our crumpled foam.

All these small, ugly,
round-shouldered, kindly-looking,
bandy-legged, shrivelled,
concave-chested beings had
affairs of their own in mind.

The train came to rest and disgorged its 200 passengers

Their cry is impressive and melancholy. They draw incredible loads

Yokohama does not improve on further acquaintance

I receive much warning and dissuasion

New sounds to greet me:
the combined clatter of those
400 neat clogs.

The two men who pull
press brown hands and thighs against
a heavy cross-bar.
Uphill their mates behind shove
with their thick smooth-shaven skulls.

Harmoniously
dull: grey sky, grey sea, grey roofs—
a dead-alive look.

As to fleas which are
the curse of travelling, sleep
in a bag drawn tight
round the throat, or smear your skin
thickly with carbolic oil.

The runners wore straw sandals which had to be replaced twice
on a journey of 23 miles

This magnificent avenue must lead to something grand and beautiful
like itself

We were among the foothills at a height of 1000 feet

I never saw people take such delight in their offspring

Blue and white towels hung
from the shafts: sweat ran down their
lean brown tattooed backs.

Those stone effigies
of Buddha and disciples
though defaced (mostly)
or tumbled down, gaze upon
the passing world benignly.

The dash and tumble
of a thousand streams shouting
applause to grey skies.

Fathers holding sons,
mothers instructing daughters,
children cradling dolls
(the ghosts of past loves bearing
spirit babies in their arms).

The hard day's journey ended in an exquisite yadoya

In one hangs a kakemono of a blossoming branch of the cherry on white silk

...whose beautiful foliage is as common as the bramble is with us

Bad roads and bad horses detracted from my enjoyment

A smiling girl brought
plum-flower tea, bean curd and a
lacquer bowl of snow.

Which of itself fills
the whole room with sweet freshness.
Its artist painted
nothing but cherry blossoms,
and fell in the rebellion.

Blue hydrangea
the very blue of heaven—
yellow raspberries.

Day's end. Still, hot rain;
the air stifling, electric;
horseflies tormented
and the men and horses crawled.
And the men and horses crawled.

When I arrived a whole bevy of nice looking girls took flight

The crowd was filthy beyond description. Why should the
'quiver' of poverty be so full?

...through rice-fields varying from 30 yards square
to a quarter of an acre

Do you remember a sentence in Dr McGregor's last sermon?
'What strange sights some of you will see!'

Straw hat, unshaven
eyebrows and unblackened teeth?
A foreigner.... Run!

Naked, old fashioned
children: born to be bitten
by vermin and pressed
like their fathers for taxes;
soil, toil their inheritance.

on the tops of dykes
dwarf beans are planted, their red
flowers shake in the wind.

Could there be a stranger
than a decent looking man
lying on his chest,
intently reading a book,
clothed only in spectacles.

*Five policemen dispersed them; but they had hardly disappeared
when the crowd gathered again*

*The teahouse almost hanging over the knife-edge ridge
of the pass*

The Rhine without its ruins, and more beautiful

*A broad full stream winding marvellously through
a wooded country*

Shuffling in their clogs
1000 people sound like
a hailstorm's clatter.

As we reached the house
a vast zigzag of blue flame
illuminated
outside and in: folk crowded
round a hearth. Pitch black again.

Mountains connected
by grey ridges no broader
than a horse's back.

Except the boatman
and myself, no one's awake
all the hot silent
afternoon—so dreamy and
delicious to float downstream.

The town would afford a good lesson to the Edinburgh authorities

*I wished that some of the most staid directors of the Edinburgh
Medical Missionary Society
could see him!*

And out we go again…

The houses have very steep roofs of shingle, weighted with stones

So well swept and clean
I hesitate to walk here
in my muddy boots.

Dr Palm coming
home from an expedition
with a tandem of
naked coolies racing
over the barren ridges.

Under the fir-trees
merciless-ly jolted. Twi-
light: a s-single house.

When snow lies thick here
the deep verandahs form one
sheltered promenade.
No poverty appears then:
rich folk, too, go robed in white.

No encouragement is ever given, but we get on, and shall get on,
I doubt not

'The Flowing Invocation' (a piece of cotton suspended just above
a quiet stream)

Lines of poetry hung up... I have several times been asked to write
something for display

The entire police force of Japan numbers 23,300

'Unbeaten tracks?' 'Och,
an awful mountain road.'
'Washout!' 'Rocks. No go.'

Pour water through cloth;
let it drip: for a mother
drowned deep in Blood Lake
can hear her baby crying.
Once this cloth wears through…she's free.

Komatsu Sunday—
not a day of rest for me:
frogs croaking all hours.

Educated men
in the prime of life—and if
30 per cent of them do
wear spectacles, this does not
detract from their usefulness.

At Nikko I asked him how many wives a man
could have in Japan

An 'infant prodigy', a boy of four with the dignified
demeanour of an elderly man

Torrents of rain were still falling

When the white mists parted

'One lawful wife, but
as many more as he can
pay for—like England.'

Self-possessed in silk,
a dark striped blue kimono,
don't insult him with
toys—the monster's taught himself
to read and write poetry.

Dripping horses steamed.
Between mud-splashed persimmons
we slid down the hill.

Lichen-covered stumps;
the damp, balsalmy smell of
cryptomeria;
tawny currents dashing through
this glen in gusts of passion.

Thus came the phrase 'Thy word is a light unto my feet'

Tumbling and stumbling
I was helped by his strong arm
bearing a lantern.

Notes

BACK TO THE WALL

'Time of Fever', 'Release of Prisoners' and 'Anniversary' are recalled
from my pamphlet *Cloud Pibroch* (2010). 'Nights' mirrors 'Days' by
Philip Larkin.

WRITING THE ASYLUM

The Writing the Asylum project is based on digitised records for
Gartnavel Hospital in Glasgow and sponsored by the University
of Glasgow Medical Humanities research group and the Wellcome
Trust. 'The Height and Depth of It' refers to Edwin Morgan's poem
'A Sunset' from *Hold Hands Among the Atoms* (1991: 48). This
mental hospital was divided into a comfortable West Wing for
paying patients and a more basic East Wing for 'paupers'.

BLUE

'Blue's Anatomy' is shaped from the Journals of Gerard Manley
Hopkins. The child in 'Peerie Poet' became George Mackay Brown.
'Like Grass Blades' is based on two letters of Edwin Morgan (see
*Edwin Morgan: The Midnight Letterbox. Selected Correspondence
1950–2010* (2015): 102–103 and 110–111). Quotations from Hugh
MacDiarmid's *The Kind of Poetry I Want* (1961) are indicated in
'Easter: The Esk'. 'Solway Elegy' was written for Kirkpatrick Dobie,
who took up poetry in retirement and published several admired
collections about his home town and its people. 'With Finnian at
His Bright House' imagines the impact of the person generally
known as St Ninian on the ancient Gaelic culture of Galloway.

MAKING TRACKS

'Approaching Summer' alternates modern haiku form with the
more ancient five-line tanka, from which it emerged. It also tries to
approach the landscape of an older Japan by following the path of a
Victorian woman traveller. Isabella Bird lived from 1831 until 1904,
and during the latter half of her life began to travel energetically
for the sake of her health. Insomnia, back problems and depression
largely disappeared as she ranged through Australia, Hawaii, the
Rocky Mountains, Japan, Tibet, Persia, Kurdistan and China,
keeping in touch by letters home to her sister. On these were
based several travel books, published by John Murray from the
1870s onwards. *Unbeaten Tracks in Japan* (1880) was re-issued by
Virago in 1984, and my sequence has its origins in her description
of that journey.

Acknowledgements

Thanks are due to the editors of journals in which some of these poems first appeared, occasionally in a slightly different form: *Dreich, Long Poem Magazine, New Writing Scotland, Painted, spoken, Shearsman, The Dark Horse* and *Words*. I am obliged to the editors of the following anthologies which presented work included here: *The Sound of Our Voices* (1999), *All Becomes Art* (2022), *The Leaves of the Years* (2022) and *All Along the Edge: Contemporary Voices Explore the Roman Frontier* (2023). Some poems originally appeared online at Clish, St Mungo's Mirrorball and World Poetry Movement Scotland.

Finally, I remain happily indebted to the creative energies of Sheila Wakefield, Founder and Editor at Red Squirrel Press and Gerry Cambridge, vital presences for poetry in Scotland. I am more than grateful to two further poet-publishers, Hamish Whyte and Richard Price, for their encouragement over many years. Without the love and support of my own family, of course, not much at all would be worth writing home about.

A NOTE ON THE TYPES

The text of this book is set in Adobe Jenson Pro, Robert Slimbach's contemporary redrawing of an original cut by Nicolas Jenson in the fifteenth century in Venice. Its graceful italic is from an original by Arrighi that followed a half-century later. It is a highly readable text typeface with a slightly sculptural look. Titles are in Jenson Pro Light and section titles in LITHOS PRO, a distinctive companion face that complements the serif.